D1406551

PICTURE STORIES FOR CHILDREN

PICTURE STORIES FOR CHILDREN

A Rebus

IRMENGARDE EBERLE

The Jefferson-Madison
Regional Public Library
Charlottesville, Virginia

DELACORTE PRESS/NEW YORK

J
Eberle
Cop 1

Published by
Delacorte Press
1 Dag Hammarskjold Plaza
New York, N.Y. 10017

Copyright 1921 by Frederick A. Stokes Company

Copyright renewed 1949 by Irmengarde Eberle

All rights reserved. No part of this book may be reproduced or
transmitted in any form or by any means, electronic or mechanical,
including photocopying, recording, or by any information storage
and retrieval system, without the written permission of the
Publisher, except where permitted by law.

Manufactured in the United States of America

First Delacorte printing

Designed by Lurelle Cheverie

Library of Congress Cataloging in Publication Data

Eberle, Irmengarde, 1898-1979.
  Picture stories for children.

  Summary: Five rebus tales include "The Friendly Hen,"
"Clever Mr. Seed," "Little Ant, Aunt Ant, and Uncle Ant,"
"Pliff, the Pixy," and "About Sonnie Rabbit's Ears."
  1. Rebuses. 2. Children's stories, American.
[1. Rebuses. 2. Short stories] I. Title.
PZ7.E18Pi 1984 [E]
ISBN 0-385-29340-2

Library of Congress Catalog Card Number: 84-4352

To
LITTLE CHILDREN
WHO ARE NOT TOO OLD TO SIT
ON SOMEONE'S LAP

CONTENTS

PAGE

THE FRIENDLY HEN 1

CLEVER MR. SEED 19

LITTLE ANT, AUNT ANT, AND UNCLE ANT . . . 39

PLIFF, THE PIXY 59

ABOUT SONNIE RABBIT'S EARS 81

THE
FRIENDLY
HEN

I

THE FRIENDLY HEN

HERE was once a 🐔 who was very friendly and very happy. She liked very much to sit on people's 🏠s and did so whenever she could get out of her pen. She liked, also, the kitchen 🚪 and always stayed as near it as possible. Every day she laid one pretty white 🥚 in a 📦 in the

3

The Friendly Hen

 The 👨👩👩 she worked for

always took it away.

Usually she did not mind letting

them take her 🥚 because the nice

👩 from the 🏠 always came out

to give her (and the other 🐔🐔 too)

🌽 twice a day. It made the little

🐦 feel very much as you feel

when someone gives you cookies—

nice brown, round ones, so— 🍪🍪🍪.

The Friendly Hen

One day the little 🐔 woke up cross. She had probably got up on the wrong side of her pole. The other 🐔🐓🐔 stayed out of her way, her temper was so bad. When the nice 👩 came to feed her, the 🐔 was not as cordial to her as usual. She did not get under her 👢 once, and she did not sit on the edge of her 🪣 and peck grains of 🌽 out of her

The Friendly Hen

. She was thinking about , she just couldn't keep from thinking about . And when the took her out of the she got crosser than ever and nearly pecked her. The scolded her and went into the very quickly. She said, "Elisabeth May," (that was the 's name) "I should be ashamed of myself to be such a cross-patch."

But the little friendly 🐔 did not think she was a cross-patch, and so she could not be really properly ashamed. She sat on the edge of the 📦 for a long time and thought, and then she quite suddenly and unexpectedly had an idea. Tomorrow instead of laying her 🪺 in the 📦 she would slip out of the hole in the 🔲 and run along the garden [illustration] and out into the woods

beyond, and here she would lay her

[illustration] where she could hide it in the

deep [illustration] in the shadow of the big

[illustration]. When she had made up her

mind about that she forgot all about

being cross, and she went out into

the barn-yard again and cackled and

squawked around as friendly as

ever. The other [illustration] were very

glad, because, though her voice was not very beautiful, it was at least much better than when she was cross.

The next morning the little brown-gray got up early while the other were still asleep. The woke her with his crowing, and then when he was taking another "last nap" she slipped out without anyone's knowing it. She ran out of the [image] of the little [image] and through the hole in the [image] and across the garden where the [image] and [image] grew—and she did not stop to eat a single [image]. She hurried right past everything and ran straight to the woods.

She found a lovely place for a nest, and here she laid her pretty

The Friendly Hen

. She liked it very much in the woods and so she stayed several days. There were plenty of and s at this time of the year so she did not miss the . Then one day she counted her and found that there were seven. And she sat right down on them and started to hatch them. She thought it very nice to be a and so she

wanted her dear, precious to

be  too.

She was such a patient little

! Oh, so much more patient

than you or I or the child next door

could ever be. She sat on her

for twenty-one days, so still

and so quiet that not even the black-

knew she was there. She

hardly ever even got up for food

except when she was unusually hungry.

The [people] in the [house] and all of

the little [hen]'s relatives and friends

thought that some wild animal had

eaten her up, and were very sorry.

The nice [women] often looked sad

and said "Poor little friendly [hen]! I

wonder what killed her."

And the [hens] talking in the

shade of the big [tree] on hot afternoons would say, "My, but isn't it a shame that little friendly 🐔 got eaten up," and "I miss little friendly 🐔 awfully, don't you?" and many other sad things.

Then one day as they lay in a cool place ruffling the dust up into their 🪶, they all jumped up at once, astounded! They had heard the little friendly 🐔's voice. And there she was coming through a hole in the ████ .

And what do you think she had with her? One tiny, little, yellow, baby chick; so tiny— 🐤 . All the 🐔🐔 ran to meet her, and the 🐓 flapped his 🪶🪶 and crowed a lovely wel-come-home-again crow. They asked where she had been and everything else all at once, and the little 🐓 told them everything as fast as she could, while the baby 🐤 stood first on one 🐤 and then on the other and waited, and got tired and impatient, and peeped, and wondered what it was all about. All the grown up 🐓🐓🐓 thought the baby 🐤 the cunningest thing they had ever seen. And the rest of the season they played with it and petted it all the time. The little 🐤 liked it very much.

The Friendly Hen

When the nice [woman] came down from the [house] with the [pail] of [corn] the little [hen] thought she would scold her for having run away, but she did not.

She was so glad to have the little [hen] back all safe and so delighted about the fluffy little baby [chick] she nearly cried. She picked them both up and ran into the [house] and showed them to all the other [people]. And so little

The Friendly Hen

friendly was even happier and

friendlier than she had been before.

CLEVER MR. SEED

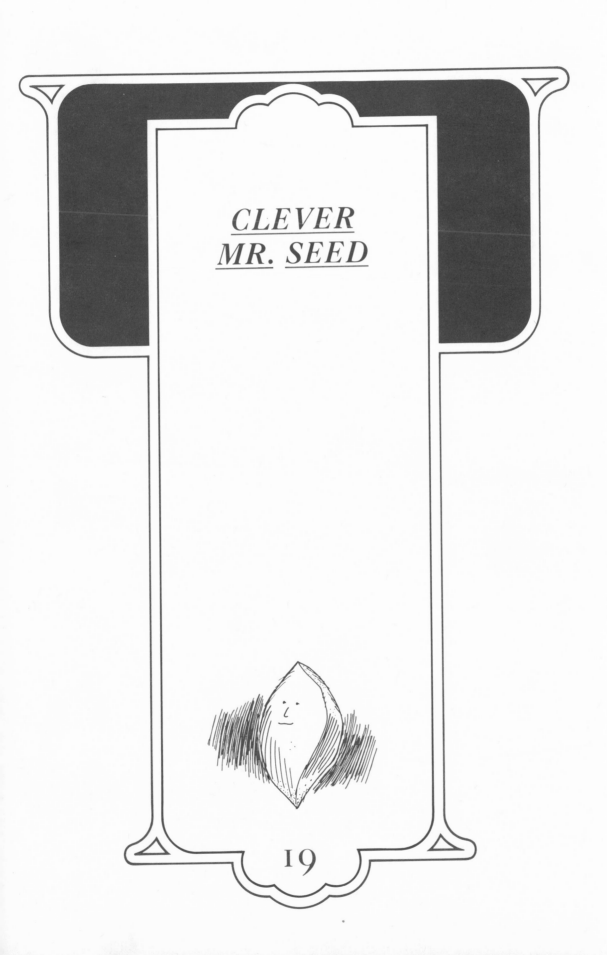

THIS is Mr. Seed—🌰. All winter he did not have any 💪 or 🦵 because he did not need them. He is a very little fellow. And he lives in a tiny 🏠 way under the ground. Last year he was a part of a 🌼 but in the autumn he went off to live by himself. He was sleepy and did not want to be disturbed.

Clever Mr. Seed

This is the 🏠 he lived in last winter. I think it is very cunning. It has a tiny 🚪 and tinier 🪟 🪟. Inside there is the smallest kitchen with a 🔥, a 🪑 and one 🪑 in it. He does not need any more than one 🪑 because he lives all alone and no one ever comes to tea.

There is a 🗄 with one ☕ and one 🥣 and one 🍽 and one 🍴 and

one ⎜ and one ⎨ in it. They are so

little that you and I could not see

them without the help of a .

His little is just barely big

enough so that his would not stick

out, if he had any. And this is where

Mr. spent all of his time all winter

long, with his little sleepy on the

softest little white .

For a long time he did not use his

and things at all. How could

he when he was fast asleep?

Then one morning someone knocked

on the of his little . It

woke him, and at first it made him

cross. He looked like this , but he

did not open his . He only turned

over in his and went back to

sleep.

But the knocking kept on and on,

most persistently. At last Mr. 🜂

really woke up, and to his own sur-

prise he felt most cheerful, and looked

like this 🜂. He thought he would

like to get up. And as he lay there

thinking about that he began to

stretch and stretch—and suddenly he

found that he had stretched until he

had little 🜂 and 🜂. (They

were roots, but he did not know it.)

25

The Jefferson-Madison
Regional Public Library
Charlottesville, Virginia

Clever Mr. Seed

He opened his 👁️👁️ wide and wondered at himself.

At first he did not know what to do with these new things. That was not strange, for he had never had any 🦵 and 🦵 before. He was just thinking how nice they were when the knocking started again. This time not only on the 🧱 of his 🏠, but also on the 🚪 and the ⊞ ⊞. (It was the spring rain, but he did not know anything about rain.) He was so surprised that he jumped out of 🛏 with his brand new 🦵 before he knew it. And that is how he found out what to do with them.

He ran to the ⊞ and peeped out, but he could see nothing; so he began to walk about and look at his little [image]. He had been nearly en-

tirely asleep when he came there in

the autumn, and so he had never

seen it. He liked the little [image] very

much. When he came to the [image]

he remembered that he was hungry,

so he went to the [image] and got out

the coffee-[image] and other things and

made his breakfast on the little [image].

He was most careful not to burn his

Clever Mr. Seed

fine new 🐾. He sat down on his

little 🪑 at his little 🪑 and drank

coffee out of his little ☕. He

thought the little 🥄 particularly nice

and so he stirred his coffee much

more than he need have.

After breakfast he felt so good that

he stretched himself again, and as he

did so his little brown 🧥 popped

open—and to his great delight he

found that he had a beautiful green

🧥 on underneath. He admired him-

self very much, and searched his little

🏠 for a mirror so that he could

see himself better. There wasn't any,

however, but when he started to wash

his 🍽️ he found out that he could

see himself in the bottom of his very

shiny little dish-🥣. And he was glad

to see what a nice looking fellow he was.

Clever Mr. Seed

When he had finished cleaning up he thought to himself, "Washing 🥣🫖 is all very well, but I do not think I should like to do it more than three times a day," and with that he sat down in his little 🪑 and put his 🦶🦶 up on the ▦-sill, like this— 🪟 .

The knocking had stopped completely now. It was getting very warm, though, for out in the open world the was shining. After a while Mr. got so warm that he decided to go outside. He opened his little very cautiously and peeped out, like this .

He smelled something so deliciously sweet out there that he popped right out of the and started to in-vestigate. All the while he sniffed with his little funny —so that he would not miss any of this wonderful sweetness. (It was spring, but he did not know it.) It was the loveliest smell he had ever dreamed of. He thought it came down from above, so he climbed up on the 🧱 of his little 🏠 and from there to the 🧱; and then he began pulling himself right up through the earth by grabbing hold of bits of rocks and things.

And it never seemed to occur to him that he was doing a most remarkable thing. It did not make him conceited at all, only very happy.

Suddenly his 🙂 stuck out of the earth and right out into the sweetest, softest yellow sunshine. And now he had a 🌱 on, a 🌱 with green plumes on it. But he was so interested in what was going on all about him that he did not notice this. He was very happy and he did not know that he didn't look at all like the Mr. 🌱 he had seen in the bottom of the shiny dish-🍲. In fact, he was not a seed at all any more, but a tiny little plant.

While he was still staring at the wonderful blue sky above him a cocky little 🐦 came by and chirped at him:

Clever Mr. Seed

"Hello! And who are you?"

"I am a 🌻 plant," he answered without hesitation.

How he knew that is more than I can tell, for only a short while ago he had been Mr. 🌱. He must have been very clever or he never could have kept track of himself through all these changes and known what to call himself when he became a plant. But he was right, he was

a sunflower plant now, and this is his

signature.

LITTLE ANT, AUNT ANT, AND UNCLE ANT

ONCE there was a little _🐛_.

He lived with his Aunt Ant and his Uncle Ant, who looked very much like this 🐜🐜. They were very much respected among the 🐜🐜🐜 because they had such especially good stings.

Aunt 🐜 and Uncle 🐜 and little 🐜 all lived together in a hole in the

ground, so— under a big

They were not the only ones that

lived there. Oh, no indeed! There

were simply thousands of other

there too. It was like a big hotel.

All the liked to work.

They just couldn't do anything else.

And consequently, they thought the

little , who did not like to work,

very lazy. The little did not

care. He did not mind being called

lazy just so long as they did not

make him work. But Uncle and

Aunt were very sorry and very

ashamed of him. Whenever they

could find two small enough

and close enough together they would

sit down on them and talk the mat-

ter over.

No matter how much they talked

they never could decide what to do with their nephew, Little ⟨image⟩. Often they would scold him, sometimes they would nearly sting him, they would be so mad.

Meanwhile Little ⟨image⟩ would be enjoying life. He would lie on a ⟨image⟩ and let the wind rock him to sleep, as if he were in a ⟨image⟩. And some- times he would hide inside of a ⟨image⟩, and when some little 👦 or 👧 would

smell it he would come out and

frighten them.

Aunt 🐜 and Uncle 🐜 got more

and more distressed about him every

single day. Nobody could think what

to do about him. He was a disgrace

to his Uncle 🐜, his Aunt 🐜 and to

the whole 🐜 race. And they all

shook their 🐜🐜🐜 and wondered

whatever would become of him.

At last the Uncle went to see the 🦉. In the woods one always goes to see the 🦉 when one doesn't know what to do about anything.

The 🦉 was high up in a tall pine 🌲—Oh, many hundred feet high—and you can imagine how long it took the 🐜 to get up there. He took his lunch along in a 🧺 and ate it when he got to the fifty-second branch, and he had to stop and rest many times more before he got to the top.

When he at last got there the was fast asleep. He called to him but his voice was too small, and the did not stir. At last, in desperation, he climbed upon the owl's and bit him in as friendly a way as he could. He knew that this was not a very nice thing to do, and felt very

much ashamed of himself, but it was

the only thing he could think of.

The did wake up then. He

wriggled his and said:

"Well, well, well, who is here?"

The was very much relieved to

see the take it so good-naturedly,

and answered immediately, calling up

to him at the top of his voice:

"I want to ask you something!"

The had closed his again and the was afraid he had gone back to sleep, but he had not.

"If you will climb up on this that is next to my ear," he said, without moving, "I shall be able to hear you better and it will at the same time save you the indignity of yelling at me."

The ⟨image⟩ did so, and immediately began telling him about his nephew, Little ⟨image⟩.

"What shall we do with him!" cried Uncle ⟨image⟩ when at last he had finished his tale; and he wiped his poor puzzled brow.

"Nothing at all, nothing at all," said the ⟨image⟩, opening his ⟨image⟩ ⟨image⟩ a wee crack. "You are mistaken, your nephew is not lazy."

"But he is!" cried the uncle desperately.

The was entirely unruffled.

"You say he is an , and you say he is lazy. In one and the same breath you contradict yourself. One of these must be wrong—he cannot be both. Go home and see which he is."

The was not at all satisfied

because he knew what he would see

if he went home—the same lazy little

child. He did not want to have

come up that tall, tall for nothing.

He spoke with the for many,

many minutes—and to an minutes

are very long. He begged and begged

for better advice, but the had

gone back to sleep.

Then Uncle climbed back and

forth along the 🌳 next to his ear and yelled at him, but the 🐨 did not turn a 🪶. Then he walked down and bit his 🐾 again, but even this did not wake the 🐨 this time. So the 🦂 bit him again— and not so kindly, because he was most annoyed, and then he ran down the 🌲 as fast as he could go.

When he got in sight of his home,

Aunt 🐜 came running down the path

to meet him, 🐜 her 🔺 flapping in

the wind and her 🐜 strings flying

behind her.

"What did he say—what does he

think . . . " she began asking him.

But Uncle 🐜 was too out of breath

to talk right away, and so they

waited until they came to the 🪑

in front of their 🏠. Here they

sat down, and then Uncle told

Aunt all that had happened.

As it happened, Little was

lying under a nearby and heard

it all. He listened especially hard

because he had great respect for the

. He heard his Uncle say:

"And then the said, 'You say

he is an , and you say he is lazy.

One of these is wrong—he can't be

both. Go home and see which he is.'"

"Umph," thought Little 🐜, "I guess I'll see which I am for myself."

And so he started right out to find a pool so that he could see himself.

When he got there he climbed upon a blade of 🌱 that bent over the pool conveniently, and then looked at himself. 🦗

What he saw there was certainly

most distinctly a little , and nothing else in the world. He looked at himself a long time to make quite sure. Then he went home, half glad and half disappointed. He was glad indeed that he was an , but he was sorry he could not be lazy, too.

As he went along the path he stumbled over a wild oat , and before he knew it he had picked it up and was carrying it home.

The was right. Little was

an and so he had gone to

work.

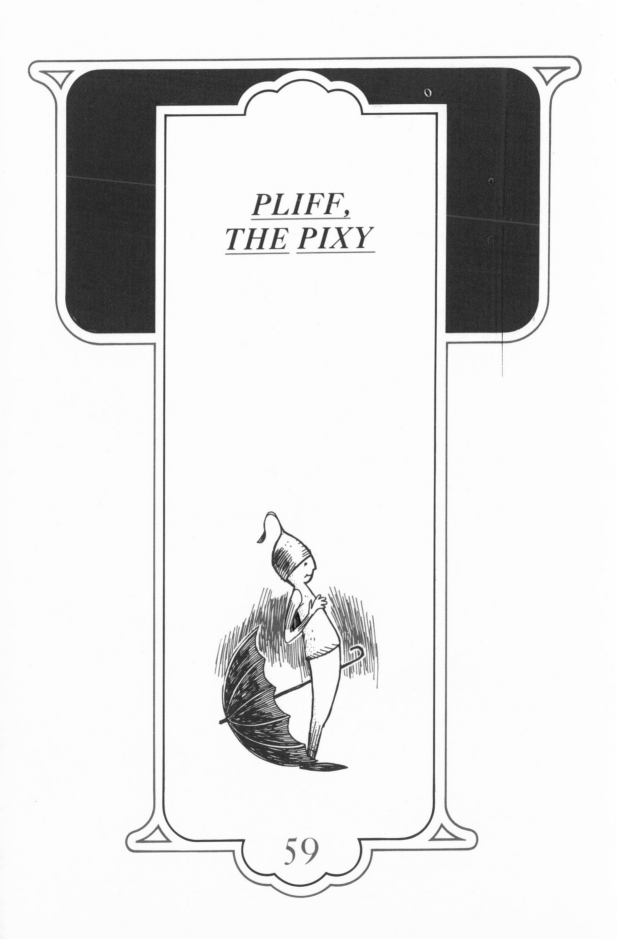

PLIFF,
THE PIXY

THIS is a story that happened a very long time ago, before the field knew what made winter and what made summer.

One cold night at the very beginning of the winter, a pixy named Pliff went out to get a little kindling for the little . His wife, Plipp, was going to make -cakes for dinner.   Here are pictures of Pliff and

Plipp , and now every time

you see those pictures you will know

whom I mean.

When was about to leave the

he said to , "I will be

back very soon and help you put our

to ." Then he put on his

, because it was raining, and

went out. called after him:

"Pliff, you are a fairly nice little 🧝,

but you always leave the 🚪

open behind you when you go out;

and you had better take your ☂."

And ☂ did.

Then he started out **again**. He had

just arrived at the corner of the 🚧

of the big field when he met a brown

field 🐭 whom his intimate friends

called Samuel. He was a cunning

little fellow and had very blinky,

bright . Samuel sounds like a

very big name that ought to belong

to some very important person, but

it did not, this time.

"How do you do, Sam," said

taking off his .

"I do not do at all," said the

sadly from beneath his ☐.

"No?" asked in surprise. He

wiped the rain-drops from his 👁 👁

and then he saw that the 🐭 looked

very sad indeed. So 🧚 asked him

what was the matter.

"My dear," said the 🐭, "I have

lost a very dear friend."

"That is certainly sad," said the 🧚,

and then they both sat down on a

🪨 and cried 🪨. But first

they chose a stone that was sheltered

from the rain. They did not like to have the water dripping down their necks.

The thought the was sadder than he himself was, because he cried so very many tears. He did not know that that was a special talent of a pixy. So when he thought that he had pretty nearly all the sympathy that he deserved, he stopped his crying and said:

"Come, we have cried enough, Pliff.

I will tell you now why we have

been crying. Do you mind if I take

off my 👢👢?"

The 🧝 shook his 👒. He did

not speak because he was using his

little ▢. Then they both took off

their 👢👢 and sat on their 🦵 kiss

to keep them warm.

Pliff, the Pixy

"It is like this," said the 🐭 ges-

ticulating with his 🐾, "All summer

long the wind and I were great

friends. He was kind and gentle and

merry, and I liked him very much.

We got to be such good friends, in

fact, that I invited him to the 🏠,

and Mrs. 🐭 and the 🐭 liked

him very much too. We all told him

to come to see us as often as he

could.   And after that he blew in

quite often.   He was always a perfect

gentleman."   And here he stopped

and wiped a great tear from his 👁,

and the 🧚 patted him on the back

🧚🐭.   Then the 🐭 went on.

"All through the summer we were

the best of friends.   In fact, the wind

used to go out of his way to do me

a favor.   Then one morning in the

late autumn I slept a little longer than usual. Perhaps it was because it was cold, perhaps because Mrs. 🧹 had not raised the 🪟. At any rate, when I did wake up I went out as usual to gather stray grains of 🌽. And what do you think happened? When I came across that hill over there, Mr. Wind, whom I had thought my friend, jumped out on me and almost blew me over. I tried to come

to an understanding with him but he

only laughed at me and began blow-

ing my hair the wrong way —

. I was so disappointed

in him that I finally went home and

cried. Mrs. cried when I told

her, and all the too. Mrs.

and I had to put them all to

, they made such a fuss. Then

we had supper.   Mrs. 🐭 put the

best cloth on the 🪑, and the best

🍵 and 🍽, and 🔪 and 🍴 and

🥄, to cheer us up.   We had just

settled down comfortably, when all of

a sudden the 🚪 burst open and in

tore the Wind! He knocked over the

🪑 and blew the 🪑🪑 we were sit-

ting on right out from under us! He

broke the 🍽 all to pieces. But

all that didn't hurt so much as having

one's best friend turn on one so. It

nearly killed us. And I have had to

block my [door] with a [rock] ever

since. And now I hardly dare to go

out at all."

"That," said the [pixy], "sounds

like a very sad story. But you are

mistaken about your friend the wind.

Your friend is not the only wind in

the world. There are many winds. The chief ones are Spring Wind, Summer Wind, Autumn Wind and Winter Wind. Your friend was perhaps Summer Wind—or probably Autumn Wind. That morning when you slept so long, you slept long because it was cold. And that night Autumn Wind had to leave for the south, and he was too kind-hearted to wake you up even to tell you good-bye."

The gave a squeak of joy.

He was so glad it was not his friend

who had done such mean things. He

got up and kissed Pliff, (brown,

blinky eyed are very affec-

tionate), and then he sat down again

and said, "My dear Pliff, you

have taken a great load from my

♡. I thank you a thousand times."

Pliff, the Pixy

"Not at all," said , bowing politely, "I must go to my now for will be wondering where I am. Besides which I am hungry."

They both started to put on their . It took the much longer because he had four . While he was finishing the opened his , and then he said:

"Samuel, I don't want to advise

you about your private affairs, but, as a friend, I must tell you that I would not associate with Winter Wind if I were you. I would go to my and go to . Your whole should do that. And I would not come out except on particularly fine days when Winter Wind takes a nap, and the shines."

"Thank you," said Samuel, "and

good night to you, Pliff." Then he went home and told Mrs. and the , and they all went to right away. They took long naps, sometimes several days long, and they got up very seldom.

And that is how field learned about the seasons of the year. It was a very long time ago that this happened. Now all know about the seasons and

no has to tell them any more.

When Pliff got near his own

again, was standing in the

with a , ringing a dinner

. This did not surprise , because

she always did this when he stayed

out unusually long. She did it so that

he could find his way home if he had

gotten lost. She was always thinking

that he might get lost, but he never did. And the never again mistook rough Winter Wind for his friend Summer Wind.

ABOUT SONNIE RABBIT'S EARS

N the [rabbit] world things are very different from things in the world of [people]. For instance, father and mother [rabbits] are very proud of their baby [rabbits] if they have long [ears]. In fact, they think the longer the [ears] the better the child. And as long as I have lived among [people] I have never heard

83

About Sonnie Rabbit's Ears

any [picture] or [picture] wish their [picture]

and [picture] had longer [picture] [picture]. Have

you?

I knew a [picture] once that had a son

who had the longest [picture] in the world.

All the [picture] in the neighborhood

agreed about that—though they hated

to say so, for they would have liked

to have had a rabbit [picture] of theirs

have the best [picture]. But these were so

About Sonnie Rabbit's Ears

especially fine they had to agree

about them. The little boy rabbit

looked like this . And he had a

most unkind way of twitching his

at the other little , which

always made their ears feel dread-

fully short. That was not very nice

of him, but his father did not notice it.

They wanted to take a picture of

the , and the little too, of

About Sonnie Rabbit's Ears

course, and as no one in the whole

community had a 🧀, they finally

had a meeting to discuss what should

be done.

One big fat 🐰 who was smoking

a 🚬 said he knew that the daugh-

ter (so— 👧) of the farmer (so— 🚶)

who lived in the 🏠 on the

hill where the cedar 🌲🌲 grew, had

a 💼. So the proud father 🐰

started right straight out for the farm.

He had never been there before, but he soon knew that he was headed in the right direction because he came to a large pen, which the fat had said he must go through. He was wondering which would be the shortest way to the , when suddenly over the top of the there appeared the most astoundingly, wonderfully, large he had ever seen! They were three or four times as large as the whole of his little son—ears and all.

He sat down on a ⌐ and cried great, sad tears 🐰. Because now his son's 🐰 were no longer the finest in the world.

The creature with the prize

looked at him very sympathetically

and finally asked:

"What are you crying about?"

The father stopped crying

just long enough to tell him:

"I thought my son had the finest,

longest in the whole world. And

now I see that you are a still finer

with still finer !"

"You are mistaken," said the creature, "My ⧘ ⧘ are indeed fine, but I am not a 🐰 but a 🫏."

The 🐸 was so glad to hear this he got up and danced. He did not know what a 🫏 was but he was glad it wasn't a 🐰.

The 🫏 thought the 🐰 very funny when he danced, and so he laughed a loud and cheerful mule laugh 🫏. It made a dreadful noise, and frightened the so

that he ran off without looking where

he was going. When he stopped for

breath, at last, he found himself right

square in front of a . And just

then it opened, and there stood a

little with a large straw on.

"Hello!" said the .

"Hello!" said the .

"Will you lend me your ?"

asked the . "I have a son with remarkably fine , and I want to take a picture of them—the ".

"Oh," said the , "how perfectly lovely! Surely you may have my ".

Then she went into the and brought the out to him.

The thanked her very much, and ran right straight back to the woods where his friends were waiting.

About Sonnie Rabbit's Ears

He did not go by the pen where the was, though — because he did not like his laughter.

When he got back to the woods all the were still waiting for him under the same . And they all complimented him on his speedy return. The father bowed in greeting, and then told them how nice the farmer was, and what a nice she lived in.

He did not mention the (he

did not think it important enough).

Then they told the young prize

to stand in the -light in a place

where they could get him with a fine

background of wild . And

after posing him many ways to see

which way the would show off to

the best advantage, they finally

were all ready to take the picture.

And what do you think! The 🐰 were so long that they would not go into the picture, no matter how those rabbits tried.

So they all put their heads together 🐰 and talked it over. And at last they determined to make the young 🐰 stand up against the flat side of a large 🌿 and ask Mr.

About Sonnie Rabbit's Ears

Woodpecker to mark the outline of

the 🐰 on the 🌿 with his very

strong 🦫.

The father 🐰 was a little tired

from his other long walk, so they sent

another 🐰 to the 🏠 of the 🦫,

to ask him if he would do them this

great favor.

Mr. Woodpecker was at home, and

as he had had a particularly good

About Sonnie Rabbit's Ears

breakfast of particularly good
and he was in a fine humor,
and said he would be more than glad
to do this for the . And he
flew right straight over and did it.

The little did not like it so
much as the others. He said it tickled
his to have the mark around
them, and he made faces like this

 But this time the father

was strict, and Sonnie had to stand very still till Mr. Woodpecker was through. And if you go to that particular wood under that particular and find that particular you will see there still the tracing of that little boy 's specially fine .

About the Author

IRMENGARDE EBERLE was born in San Antonio, Texas, in 1898. She moved to New York City in the early 1920s and began her career as a fabric designer, then worked as a writer and magazine editor. She began writing full-time in 1937 and published more than sixty books for children before her death in 1979.